AFTER *the* STORM

POST STORM STRATEGIES

DR. MICHAEL FREEMAN

FREEMAN PUBLISHING

Freeman Publishing
2261 Oxon Run Drive
Temple Hills, MD 20748
freemanpublishing@sofcc.org

Printed in the United States of America

Author photography by Clark Bailey Photography
Book cover design by Chantee The Designer LLC

Library of Congress Cataloging-in-Publication data
ISBN 978-1-944406-02-3

To my awesome wife, who stood with me through the entire storm! DeeDee you gave a new meaning to a "ride or die chic." You served as my caterer, manicurist, vision board maker, germ fighter, and nurse. When I couldn't lift a limb, you were there as my hands and feet to feed and bathe me. Your sleepless nights and tireless nursing hours will forever be appreciated. I laughed at how the nurses officially certified you as their co-worker.

And to all that stood with me in faith. I love you all and pray that God will increase you more and more.

TABLE OF CONTENTS

Introduction

After the storm, we are never the same. We are forever changed, tested, and proven. Our lives are fine-tuned and our faith is fortified. Survival mode has a way of making us cut through the fog and ambiguities to determine what is necessary and what is not. Storms are refining processes that remove excess materials, people, and expose unresolved issues. Storms can break us, reveal cracks in our foundations, or make us see ourselves stronger than we ever imagined. After surviving a great test, you have proved that you can withstand storms. Many are tempted to ease up and simply "chill" after a storm, but that is a huge mistake. Just like the world turns and fads and styles resurrect themselves, storms and strategic attacks sent by the enemy do as well. If you have been tested in an area at some point in the past, you should be prepared to perform even better when that test comes back around.

It will come back around. However, we as believers, can decree and declare that the same storm will not prevail a second time.

The Storm Series has been designed to give you strategies to defeat the enemy and hail victorious in every kind of storm. You have been equipped with pre-storm strategies to help you develop a healthy spiritual life in Before The Storm. In During The Storm, you learned how to sleep like Jesus did during your storm, based on our revisit of the storm He encountered in the gospel of Mark chapter six. In this third book, After The Storm, you will learn how to analyze what has happened to you based on six types of sight, determine who and what sent your storm, and become equipped for the next time that you have to face off with one of these attacks. When we fail to reflect on what has happened, we end up living our lives in circles. Perhaps you have found yourself in one bad relationship after the next, or maybe you know someone who constantly mismanages their finances. The reason why this happens to people is simply because people often make it through a storm (tragedy, betrayal, setback, heartbreak, or loss) and they keep moving along with life without properly analyzing why or how they ended up in that particular situation. As a result, they don't change anything and whichever open door played as the culprit - making an entryway to the storm - remains open. The enemy tests and attacks them over and over in those areas and they fall into demonic cycles of fighting for territory that they should have seized a long time ago.

There is nothing new under the sun, and you better believe that life has a way of repeating itself just like styles. We have styles and fashion statements in the earth that continuously come back around. It seems like once upon a time, straight leg pants were out of style and now they are back in style. Bell-bottoms were out of style and now you see them making their comeback—afros, big sunshades; you name it. Well, we know that the enemy has the same attacks, just presented in different packages from season-to-season and year-to-year. It behooves us to maintain the same regimen that we maintained before any storms happened in our lives. If you have not established a healthy spiritual regimen, it's your time right at this moment to start one. Once you win a storm, you then have the opportunity to examine, by the Spirit of God, what you may have not been doing and now you can incorporate all the things that He has revealed to you. You want to put this regimen in place immediately so that you win the next battle when it rears its head. I love something that my Pastor Dr. Frederick K.C. Price brought to my attention years ago. He said that when it comes to having a green luscious lawn, you don't water it with

H2O one day, diesel fuel the next day, or milk the day after that. In order to keep the grass luscious, it takes the same H2O every day. You may add to the regimen, but you should use at minimum, the same strategy each day. This is the same with your daily life with God—establish a good healthy strategy that will serve as a defense against the storms. Whether it's your praise and worship regimen, fasting and prayer, witnessing to others, your love walk, there are certain things that you should do every day. If you don't have a strategy, you can start the righteous regimen that I suggested in Before The Storm: Pre-Storm Strategies.

In this book, we will confront the difficult questions. Why did this happen? What allowed the enemy access into your life? Was it a personal sin or a sneak attack from Satan? Did you cause it or were you just a victim? Many people may ask themselves, "Why?" but won't be truthful enough to get to the bottom of things by seeking the Lord's guidance and revelation. In this book, we're going to go deep into the "Why?" and "How?" of the storm. Once you're able to thoroughly analyze and determine the root of the evil attacks on your life, you will be prepared and equipped when the next storm appears in your forecast.

Applying these lessons will save your life.

CHAPTER 1:
HOW DID THIS HAPPEN?

The tone of one who asks this question during or after a storm can often come off as self-righteous or bemoaning as if to suggest, "Why me?" or "I didn't deserve this." However, truth be told, and the truth should be told, "How?" and "Why?" are the foremost questions believers should seek to understand after surviving something that was set out to throw us off course.

When one makes it through a storm, it can be tempting to celebrate and keep moving along with life, but those who have been affected by literal storms such as recent Hurricane Harvey, Katrina, or Irma know that celebrations are short-lived. There is rebuilding to do. Storms were designed, not for celebration, but for destruction. They uproot families, cause mass evacuations, wipe out households, and leave many dead. The saying, "Your storms are designed to make you stronger," is a lie. Storms are designed to kill you, which is why it is important for us to prepare ahead of time, stand firm in faith during, and seek revelation after. Truly the enemy plots against the people of God to brew storms that will rock us to our core and destroy everything in our paths. When we overcome life's storms, it is tempting to never look back and focus on moving forward, but this is a deadly mistake. It is for this reason primarily that After the Storm is necessary.

By now you may have read the previous two books in The Storm Series: Before the Storm and During the Storm, and you know about the life-threatening storm I survived. During the summer of 2014, a storm hit my household like a hurricane and threatened to take my life— a sudden loss of breath, collapse to the floor, inability to breathe on my own, medivac to have emergency surgery, and I fell into a comma for three weeks. When I came to consciousness, I was unaware that my life had been at risk— instead, I could only recall dreams and visitations taking place. While my physical body was laid in a hospital bed, my spirit had been traveling all over the world hanging in some of the world's most prestigious places with some of the most influential people of our time. Because my spirit was in God's hands, I was as well. My wife played the Word in my ears and I even recall some of those prayers and hearing some of my favorite gospel songs even while I was unconscious. She knew what to do and so did I. Metaphorically, the faith deposits we had made up until that point sustained us during the storm. Faith is the currency of the kingdom of God—we get everything through faith, especially survival. This situation proved just how important daily faith deposits are to the life of believers. During the storms, we will need to withdraw based on what we have put in, and if you have not put anything into your faith account, there will be nothing to take out when you face those life or death situations.

In the natural world, however, this tragedy shook my immediate family and church family to the core and I know it stretched my loved ones' faith. In hindsight, I realized that faith was the surviving factor that changed the trajectory and impact this storm had on our lives. The very topic I had preached and lived for decades moved heaven and hell on my behalf. The level of faith by which I had lived deemed me a survivor. To this day, the doctors consider my story a medical miracle.

Despite this good news however, when it was all over and we were well on our way to recovery and were getting great reports from the doctors, one of the most prevailing thoughts and questions that I had was how did this happen? Everybody was enamored and excited about the victory that was wrought. If you can imagine, it was kind of difficult to want to explore and go back to look at this particular situation. I didn't want to put a damper on the victory, but I knew I had to explore this. I had always been taught that every lesson unlearned is a lesson repeated, so it behooved me to explore the door that was used to accomplish this attack in my life.   Sometimes, if we don't try to discover what we did wrong, our ignorance can play as an open invitation for a repeated scenario.

There's an exploration process that I definitely needed to go through to explore how this all happened. To do this, I had to implore my six different types of sight (see chapter two); then, I had to determine if I did anything to cause this attack like some had suggested. In other words, was this storm self-inflicted, caused by the world, or sent by Satan? These questions require deep self-reflection, life evaluation, and intimacy with God. I wanted to know, "God, how did this happen? What could I have done to circumvent this storm?" Most people don't want to admit when they are wrong or even go searching to find fault within themselves, but I honestly had to do that. This attack was too strong and too close for comfort and I could not afford not to take a deeper look into the 'How?' After the exploration process, I could truly enjoy the fruit of the storm and watch God's will according to Romans

8:28 play out in my life.

It's impossible to see the complete picture while we're living in the canvas. The how or why of a situation is revealed afterwards. For instance, if we go back to the beginning of humankind, in the Garden of Eden. Eve had no knowledge that she had encountered a storm once the snake approached her about eating from the tree of the knowledge of good and evil. She didn't realize that her one act of disobedience would have eternal implications for every other person who would walk the earth. She opened the door for Satan due to her curiosity, pride, disobedience, and greed. This is often the case with storms—not always, but often. Many people don't realize the deep impact that one small act of disobedience will have and that a storm has been released into their lives. This is true for the first-time drug user who casually tries a recreational drug at a party. This person isn't thinking about the years of addiction, countless amounts of money, and loss time this one moment will create for his future.

You can often determine how the storm entered your life by examining your pre-storm regiment, areas of vulnerability or sin, and also the timing of your attacks. In chapters three through five, we discuss the root of storms—Satan, the world, and our flesh. You may have a deeper insight on "how" a storm was able to infiltrate your life once you know who or what sent it.

"Why did this happen?" Your storm was not just about you. If it was sent by the enemy or even created by your flesh but fueled by the enemy, there is a bigger reason for the attack. Satan tempted Eve because he wanted to separate humans from God and the way to do that is through sin. He found Eve alone (mistake one) near a forbidden tree (mistake two). Do you see how this happened? When we are isolated from other believers, the enemy attacks us—often through mind games, like he did with Eve. He knows it would have been more difficult, maybe impossible, to tempt both Eve and Adam together, so he went for whom he considered the weaker link. There's also something to be said about the nature of his question to Eve. It seemed innocent, and the bible warns us in Genesis chapter 3 that the serpent was more cunning (or shrewd) than any beast that the Lord made. He asked Eve, "Did God really say you must not eat the fruit from any of the trees in the garden?" Seemed innocent right? This is how the enemy tempts us—often the question or suggestion that he presents seems innocent, but its calculated enough to plant doubt or pride, and then many believers take the bait. The danger in being tempted or deceived into a storm are so high and the potential ramifications are so great that Jesus warned His disciples, "I am sending you out like sheep among wolves. Therefore, be as shrewd as snakes and as innocent as doves" (Matthew 10:16).

Why were you attacked? If your stormed stemmed from Satan, he wasn't as concerned about that one storm. That was just one attack in a series of strategic and calculated plots from the pit of hell to take you out. The devil's hope is that with each storm you will grow more tired, angry, bitter, hopeless—sometimes he seeks to break believers little by little. And at other times, he tries to kill us with one big blow, as he had done with me. Satan's desire was to put a complete stop on your destiny through the storms he's released into your life. You have a purpose and a gift cluster that has been imparted to you by God. Satan's deepest fear is for you to step into all that God has called you to be. The storm you faced was just a vehicle used to accomplish the devil's greater act of terrorism, which is to kill, or steal, or destroy your entire life.

Let's dissect your storm completely now.

CHAPTER 2:
SEEING WITH TOTAL SIGHT

The scripture has stated that no evil will conquer you; no plague will come near your home. (Psalm 91:10). I believed that Word wholeheartedly, therefore, I wanted to know how could this type of attack find its way into my life. I had lived by faith principles and was certainly prepared for any type of storm, but there was a level of bewilderment that occupied space in my mind. Why and how did this happen? These questions led me on an exploration where I activated the six types of sight: hindsight, (normal) sight, insight, foresight, oversight, and out-of-sight.

The Apostle Paul instructs us not to think of ourselves more highly than we ought to think, but to think soberly (Romans 12: 3). The process that follows was a result of that sober thinking. I had a sense that this attack was from the enemy, yet I needed to do my own due diligence, knowing that my lifestyle of faith and worship are a threat to the kingdom of darkness. As believers, we have targets on our backs, so it's vitally important that we do everything in our power to see deeper into situations and expose the enemy's tactics. Satan, the father of lies, the king of this world hates you for various reasons, but mainly because you're a threat to his plans. The believer's lifestyle of prayer, praise, and living by faith is worship unto God, and not only that, God is pleased to receive this type of worship. As a former worship leader in heaven before he was rejected by God and casted out, Satan hates our lifestyle of worship. We have something that he could never get again—God's approval. He knows that this lifestyle of worship gives us power, and when we understand our power and that we already have defeated him, he will lose the ability to control and manipulate the children of God.

He who sins is of the devil, for the devil has sinned from the beginning. For this purpose, the Son of God was manifested, that He might destroy the works of the devil.

1 John 3:8

Satan is already defeated. He wants us to forget this, and when it's impossible to make us forget, he sends storms to whip us around and attempt to take the life God has given to us. We were made in God's image, and He gave us dominion over the earth (Genesis 1:26). When one understands his/her power, this person threatens the kingdom of darkness and its effect on the world we live in today. This brings me to why I knew that I had a target on my back and that Satan hates me with every ounce of his being because he hates Jesus. My storm felt like an attack from the pit of hell, but I still needed to do my due diligence and sulk in the lessons, if there were any to learn.

HINDSIGHT

I did my best to take on the mind of Christ and to review this situation with a sober mind. It first behooved me to look at this storm in hindsight. What happened and why? Hindsight is the ability to understand an event after it has happened. For me, of course it was the ability to see what I could have done prior to it happening. I began to search my memory for what I had been doing leading up to this storm. I think it's absolutely essential for everyone to refrain from repeating anything of this extent. In order not to repeat it, we must carefully examine what we have been through and why. The purpose and reason were primarily what I wanted to discover. I searched both my spiritual health and my physical health leading up to this attack, and I realized that I had been living a healthy life. If you were to go about exploring your storm in hindsight, you can follow that same approach.

What were you doing leading up to this incident that could have opened a doorway to the attack? No matter the type of storm that you experienced, you will always want to examine your spiritual health.

Were you activating the pre-storm strategies that we discussed in Before the Storm?

Depending on the type of storm that you experienced, you may want to also look at your lifestyle habits, who was in your crew/circle, and how you spent your time. The purpose of reviewing a storm in hindsight is again to understand what could have been done prior to the storm in order to change the outcome that you experienced or the entry of the storm in the first place.

SIGHT

The next area that I explored was "sight," which is the ability to look at something as it is. Sight is the process, power, or function of seeing. It can also mean spiritual or mental perception. In my case, I could view my storm from the perspective of where I was at the time—in the hospital and recently recovering. What was happening? What was going on around me as a result of this storm? There were things that had happened while I was in a comma that I knew were collateral damage from the storm. For instance, I heard about the handful of partners from my church who decided to leave when I was sick; I had also learned about people who attempted to get closer to my wife DeeDee, perceiving that I would not return to good health so they would be able to have some of my things. I also saw the blessings that had occurred even while I was in the hospital. My wife had an opportunity to activate her faith, finish her degree, and write a Grammy-nominated song.

I also reviewed where I was at during this storm. I saw a peaceful version of me, despite the storm. I had activated the behavior of Christ, when he slept through His storm while the disciples panicked because the waves and winds had become life-threatening. During the "sight" review process, I truly looked at things as they were. If you were to activate this "sight review," you want to do the following.

Observe things as they are. What is happening with this storm in your life right now?

Determine what type of effect it has/had in your life?

What occurred as a result of this storm?

During my sight review, I saw how my family was forced

to level up. I noticed that my team was intact and they did not waver. I realized that God had strategically placed people in my path during the storm to help him accomplish his purpose for deliverance in my life. I discussed this in detail in During The Storm. God placed a partner of Spirit of Faith Christian Center in the urgent care facility. She noticed me in the waiting room and knew I needed immediate care, because I did not look like myself. Then, my niece, whom was a physician and partner of our church, was working in the emergency room, another SOFCC partner joined forces with her to have me transported to a top hospital in the area, and God gave my daughter and wife conviction to approve a life-saving surgery for me. This is sight. I could see (with spiritual perception) how God worked for my good during the storm.

INSIGHT

Insight is the ability to look beyond what you can see and know what to do. Merriam-Webster defines this as the power or act of seeing into a situation (penetration); or, the act or result of apprehending the inner nature of things or of seeing intuitively. By nature of who I am, I have been trained in insight. This is what believers call seeing with our spiritual eyes. Insight is the act of going deeper with what you actually see. So in addition to seeing things as they were (discussed above) I saw deeper. I thought about the timing of this storm. Why did Satan send this storm at this time? For starters, I was home alone, and usually I'm with my wife and my home is filled with children, grandchildren and visitors. Being alone was an opportune time for Satan to attack. I want to sidebar for a moment, to expand on a bigger concept that I mentioned earlier. Satan always wants to get believers alone. Remember 1 Peter 5:8 tells us to be alert and of sober mind. Your enemy the devil prowls around like a roaring lion looking for someone to devour. Now lions are an interesting creature. They typically can be found in a large group (called prides) of about thirty lions. Within the prides, males are usually protectors who guard the prides while females are the hunters. Now these female lions usually hunt at night, and their hunting technique consists of female finding prey who are often faster than them. Because they aren't as quick as the prey they want to devour, these lionesses work as a team. They spread out and form a semi-circle (I imagine one that goes unnoticed to the prey). The younger female lions lure the prey into the circle and larger-stronger-faster female lions take the prey down. Now, the lion's roar is quite powerful and strong and can be heard up to five miles. So if our enemy, Satan, prowls around like a roaring lion, it tells me that he also operates in a herd (with lower level demons). And when he catches a pray—believers—he roars and other demons latch on to take believers down. Have you noticed that storms or attacks from Satan never come as one single problem? When you lose a job, you often deal with other issues such as financial loss, depression or self-esteem issues, weight gain, etc. This is because the pride of lions has attacked you once the hunter lion was able to take you down.

Alright now, let's get back to insight. In addition to the timing of the attack, I looked deep at the timing as it related to God's plan for my life. God had assured me of familial growth and ministry growth —and at the time, I thought the latter would be in the form of Faith City—a campus for the Spirit of Faith Christian Center and surrounding neighbors to worship God through our lifestyles, and a place that would be a central meeting area for our partners throughout the Washington-Baltimore areas. Through insight, I realized that the enemy wanted to halt those plans. I could also go deeper and look into the lives of my family. I had raised my children to value themselves sexually. My eldest daughter was married with children, however, my youngest daughter was not yet married. Our desire was to see the same promise carried out in her life. I knew that God would not allow me to be taken from here without His promises manifesting in our lives. However, because these promises would bring more glory and honor to the kingdom, I realized that the timing of Satan's storm was designed to take me out prior to the next level of anointing and blessings manifesting in our lives. That next year, after I made it out of the storm, my youngest daughter was married as a virgin and her lifestyle of faith made news headlines around the world, and she continued the church body's mission to make Jesus famous among her age group and mine too. Satan would have loved to take me out before that happened. I really hope you're following me here. If you want to activate the process of seeing your storms through insight, you should.

1. Examine the storm with a spiritual perspective.

2. Look at the timing of the attack. Why did the storm come at this time in your life?

3. What promise(s) did this storm threaten?

4. Or, what promise/process did you abandon that may have invited the storm?

FORESIGHT

Foresight is the process of seeing something before it happens. It is the act of looking forward. We hear about foresight all the time. It is commonly known as vision. What do you see? As I sat there in recovery, rehabilitating from what could have been a debilitating storm, I saw the hand of God on my life. I saw miracles taking place. I saw healing manifesting through my body. I saw God using this storm to lead massive amounts of believers to Christ. It had already begun. I saw (or heard about) a glimpse as I learned of the people my wife witnessed to in the waiting room. Later, the foresight I tapped into came to pass little by little. I tapped into foresight to envision the books, sermon series and in-person witnessing that would come about as a result of this storm. The process of foresight can also include preparation for the next storm, (which is why these books were birthed). I received a revelation that many people are ill-prepared for storms, because they have not grasped the notion that there will always be another storm. You may say, 'I beat cancer. I'm a survivor,' not realizing that arthritis or a sudden illness of another family member is on the horizon. In order to activate foresight, you should:

1. Envision how you will use the storm for God's glory.

2. Believe that God wants to elevate you spiritually and often physically.

3. Have the sense to prepare for the next storm, and the next one after that.

You don't know what the next storm or mountain-top experience will be, but you are smart enough to know, through foresight, that both are coming. What areas are vulnerable to storms—your finances, spirituality, family relationships, intimate partner relationship, business/career? Make these areas storm proof ahead of time.

So all of us who have had that veil removed can see and
reflect the glory of the Lord. And the Lord--who is the
Spirit--makes us more and more like him as we are changed
into his glorious image.
2 Corinthians 3:18

The scripture says that we go from glory to glory. Meaning, in Christ we will go from one glorious place to the next—this truth fed my faith that there was another glorious place for me after the storm. I could see it even before it happened—foresight.

OVERSIGHT

Oversight is an interesting type of sight. By one definition, it means inadvertently missing or overlooking something. For instance, if you are creating a financial report and you come up with a budget that seems accurate, only you inadvertently missed one-line item. This would be called an oversight. The other definition means regulatory supervision or care. I define oversight as the ability to see pass others' views of how a situation should be. This is similar to foresight, except you actually possess that which you have oversight over. For example, during my storm, I was considered to be on life support; then the doctors said surgery was a "last ditch" effort; then once I made it out of that, they said it would be a "miracle" if I ever walked or talked correctly again. In their world, these things may have been true, but the Freeman family had a type of oversight despite the view the doctors painted. We didn't need to know that surgery was a "last ditch" effort, because my family had heard from God and He said it was the only effort needed. You get it? So it was fine that this was a "last ditch effort" because God didn't require or need another one after that. Additionally, God was in the miracle-making business so the doctors saying that it would be a "miracle" for me to walk or talk like normal ever again was not a big deal—it was a faith challenge to expect a miracle. Now, don't get me wrong, for people without oversight or foresight into the spiritual realm, they may consider this type of "miracle" a big deal. I knew that the One who had oversight (regulatory supervision) had already deemed me healed. Remember I told you I needed to see things from Christ's perspective during and after this storm? We activated our oversight (ability to see beyond their view of the situation) to agree with God on these matters.

Activating your oversight is an authority that all believers have access to, but few use. You've probably heard me say, "What you focus on will expand." Or in application, "the glass is half empty/half full" metaphor. These are both true. Depending on your foresight, you will see one or the other—a half empty glass or a half full glass. This of course depends on whose vision you are buying into, God's or the adversary's. In order to activate foresight, you should.

1. Rely on the promises, revelations, and Word of God.

2. Don't allow the voices and opinions to deter you from those things.

3. Work like your foresight is in sight.

4. After your storm, attempt to see your situation as God sees it. There is nothing too hard for God. He has complete and ultimate oversight.

OUT OF SIGHT

Finally, brethren, whatever things are true, whatever things
are noble, whatever things are just, whatever things are
pure, whatever things are lovely, whatever things are of
good report, if there is any virtue and if there is anything
praiseworthy—meditate on these things.

Philippians 4:8

Out-of-sight is a slang term for wonderful or excellent. If you examine and put all of the various types of sight together your reality will be out of sight. You will have the ability to possess the exceeding abundantly above all you could ever think if you properly look at all the sights. Not one place in my explaining of the sights did you ever see where I agreed with the enemy in any matters concerning my storm. Upon review and through activating these sights, I grew stronger in Christ. Again, I'll repeat a point that I wrote about in During the Storm. I didn't need to go through this type of health-related storm to know that God is a healer. I knew that already based on what the Word says. However, experiencing and surviving this storm fortified what I already knew. I learned absolutely from the storm. I learned nothing about who God is, but I learned who people are. Sometimes people argue that God sends storms to test us. And if that is true, I say, why did Jesus rebuke the storms when they arose in His life if they were sent by His Father? I received a deeper revelation recently. During a Wednesday night bible study, my brother and associate Pastor DeWayne Freeman was explaining the test of Abraham, when God told him to sacrifice Isaac. See, God didn't "test" Abraham, to see what he would do. He tested, as in proved that Abraham would do what God had put in him to do. Imagine it like this, as my brother explained. You have a water bottle. If you punch a hole in the water bottle, you know that water will come out because that is what was in inside of it. However, if you open the water bottle, pour the water out and replace the contents with soda, and then punch a hole in the bottle, you know that soda will come out. How? Because you remember what you put it in. This is how God works. When we are tested by the enemy or by life or he tells us to do something (like a test) that He gave Abraham, God isn't testing us to see what we're made of, he allows a thing to prove to us what we're made of. He knows how we will respond, because He already knows what is in us. Our response is simply letting us and the devil know how we will respond and what we are made of. Our responses are no surprise to God.

It's important to activate the six types of sight and keep an out-of-sight vision after a storm, because your response is proving

CHAPTER 3:
STORMS FROM THE PIT OF HELL

In activating the six types of sight and checking the various areas from where attacks can stem (Satan, the world, or ourselves), I was certain that there was nothing I could have done for the storm to be self-inflicted. I was eating right, working out, and getting a tremendous amount of rest. During that time, I would sleep for eight to nine hours a day and I fed my body a tremendous amount of supplements as well. I had been experiencing some breathing challenges for quite some time, however, based on what the doctor said, there was nothing that I could have been doing to contribute to the attack on my body that I experienced.

There are some attacks that are sent by Satan himself directly from the pit of hell and they have nothing to do with what we've done; instead they are due to a demonic attack placed on our lives. Jesus said in John 10:10 that the devil, the enemy, Satan only comes to steal, kill and destroy and that's his m.o. (modus operandi). That's his particular job—that's what he's assigned to do. That's his mission and plan, to kill us, steal our stuff, and destroy our lives. Some attacks stem from the onslaught of this m.o.—the pits of hell. Unfortunately, Satan has the ability and the right to attack us until the day that Jesus returns.

I realized that the storm in my life did not come from God, the world, nor myself, and therefore, by process of elimination alone, it had to come from Satan. Unfortunately, there are different denominational and philosophical beliefs that people have that would suggest that God put things like this in our lives. But we know from scriptures that God will not test or tempt anyone with evil. This misnomer is derived from the Job episode where this attack came in Job's life and we see Satan himself roaming to and fro in the earth; this passage also describes God actually talking with Satan about his servant Job. God said, "Have you considered my servant Job?" Based on that scriptural reference, a lot of people are under the misunderstanding and the false understanding that God was behind the attack. But when you read the scriptures, there was a hedge that God put around Job; The hedge was removed because of the fear Job lived in, but God knew how Job would respond. Remember, God is omniscient so even His mention of

Job suggests that God knew how Job would react under the satanic attacks. Still, if we read further, there's also evidence to suggest that Job's own actions enabled Satan to attack him.

What I feared has come upon me;
what I dreaded has happened to me.
Job 3:25

In this passage Job admits that he had been thinking about—and not only that—he had feared that type of attack. This scripture gives us an understanding that Job's fear was responsible for the hedge being removed from his life. Fear is an entryway for the enemy to bring storms in our lives, because everything is accomplished through faith. Perhaps God removed the protection to show Job that he had nothing to fear.

My lungs were attacked and the enemy tried to take the breath out of my body by attacking my ability to breathe and receive oxygen. In full disclosure, prior to the attack, there were times when thoughts would come to my mind about the consistent cough that I would have while I was teaching, preaching and exercising. Many people would inquire about why I was coughing so much and so often. To be frank and candid, I would think about something bad happening. The thought would come to my mind about something going wrong. I think it was an alert from Holy Spirit Himself, however, with these thoughts, I still did not fear. Based on the Word, I knew what to do with thoughts that came that were not from God; 2 Corinthians 10:5 tells us to cast down imaginations, and every high thing that exalts itself against the knowledge of God, and bring into captivity every thought to the obedience of Christ. Even though I would have thoughts, I would hear people say, "You better go check that out." Every time I encountered a new person who heard that cough, they would have some new remedy—a grandmother's remedy like chicken soup, ginger, and the likes. I heard so many old wives' tales. People would find joy in potentially coming up with the remedy for my situation. Nevertheless, that was something that never subsided. The cough went on and on and on. I was in perfect health, aside from this cough, and I was sure to monitor it the way I should have. So when those thoughts would come to mind, I would knowingly cast them down, confessing the Word over my life, confessing over my breath and my lungs. And I would praise God for the length and number of my days and health and happiness was my confession. In casting down thoughts of fear or other ungodly meditations, you take hold of fear and anything that is operating against the will of God.

I knew this storm was not sent by God. Illness to the point of near death is not Godly at all, but unfortunately, a lot of people think that God works in concert with Satan to get people to submit their will to His will as if God and Satan are in alignment. God doesn't use sickness, depression or any other negative act to get us to comply to His will. The bible says that the love of God gets our attention. God isn't going to put us in jail cells, hospital beds or bankruptcy court to get us to love Him. I will not or ever subscribe to that doctrine, because the bible says that every good and perfect gift comes from God (James 1:17), not every mean and evil thing. I heard so many things relating to this sickness. Some suggested that my attitude or "arrogance" brought on this attack in just the same way Job's "friends" accused him. However, a doctor confirmed what I suspected, "There's nothing medical that we have discovered that has caused this to come to your life. We've checked viral and bacterial issues. There's nothing in our records that would cause us to know where this was coming from." He was a spirit-filled doctor, and he spoke to me from a medical perspective and as a believer. He said, "I know exactly where this came from. Satan devised a plan to destroy you. This was an attack from the pit of hell."

I was confident that I knew how to handle those types of attacks, through praying, fasting, declaring the Word and seeking the united prayers of intercessors. This is exactly how you will fight attacks from the pit of hell after you discern that this is what you're dealing with.

A key factor in winning the righteous fight is also following the will of God. People are often left baffled by storms and unsure if these attacks were truly from the pit of hell or if they themselves somehow brought them on. Here's what I mean. My lungs were attacked and oxygen had stopped flowing at a healthy rate. Now, as I mentioned, I took good care of myself by monitoring the issue, staying active, and getting regular check-ups with my physician. Let's imagine another type of reality however. What if I had been smoking, failing to exercise, and had not maintained my regular medical visits? If that was the reality, one could argue that I had brought the attack on myself. It would be unclear whether my actions or an assignment from the enemy was at cause. Believers are often so accustomed to God's mercy – dodging bullets because God saved them from Satan's wrath—that many people aren't living by the standards God set forth. To ensure that we are guarded at all times, we should not only practice spiritual (laws) principals, but we must also live right according to God's standard while also not violating physical laws.

His divine power has given us everything we need for a
godly life through our knowledge of him who called us by
his own glory and goodness. Through these he has given us
his very great and precious promises, so that through them
you may participate in the divine nature, having escaped
the corruption in the world caused by evil desires.
For this very reason, make every effort to add to your
faith goodness; and to goodness, knowledge; and to
knowledge, self-control; and to self-control, perseverance;
and to perseverance, godliness; and to godliness, mutual
affection; and to mutual affection, love. For if you possess
these qualities in increasing measure, they will keep you
from being ineffective and unproductive in your knowledge
of our Lord Jesus Christ. But whoever does not have them
is nearsighted and blind, forgetting that they have been
cleansed from their past sins.
2 Peter 1:3-9

Through the high treason that was committed by Adam and Mrs. Adam, we now are exposed to the attacks and onslaughts of the enemy, and Satan owns this world system. The good news is that God has given us everything according to 2 Peter 1, and this is what you need to place emphasis on at this particular time. It's so important that you read through the scripture above and know that it has already happened (past tense). God has given us everything, not some things, but everything that obtain to life and godliness. In John 10:10, it says that Satan has come to steal, kill and destroy, but Jesus has come that we may have life and have it more abundantly. With giving us life, Jesus has also equipped us with weapons for warfare. While the deceiver and accuser Satan may have free reigns in the earth, we have been given every auxiliary to overcome the attacks of the enemy. God has given us dominion. He has given us His name, His Spirit, His blood, His Son, His angels, and everything that we will ever need to overcome.

HELL'S COVERT OPERATIONS

You may not always notice the attacks and storms when the enemy releases them. You can be living life like everything is fine, not realizing you are in the middle of a storm. Let me illustrate it for you:

Imagine the faithful employee, let's call her Susan, who

has worked at a private corporation for twenty to thirty years. This person believes that she is fully vested, meaning in each pay check the company has been investing money in a retirement fund for her. After twenty years, that retirement fund should be pretty hefty with at least six, maybe seven figures. A week before Susan retires, a news story breaks about her employer. Words like FRAUD, EMBEZELLMENT, SCAM, flash across her screen. The next day, federal agents storm into Susan's job and shuts everything down, confiscates computers and business files, and instructs everyone to go into a conference room. Susan learns that not only are her employers being accused of theft, fraud, an embezzlement, but also to her disbelief lying. The funds that were supposedly going into employee retirement accounts have "disappeared." Twenty years of investment down the drain and Susan's security blanket is pulled from under her in less than twenty-four hours. You could have done everything right and in the end lose at no fault of your own. At no fault of your own, you encounter a storm.

While this may be an extreme case, storms like this happen every day. The enemy has used someone to deceive and take advantage of unknowing people, and unbeknownst to these victims, they've been in the eye of the storm. The bible describes the Holy Spirit as our intercessor praying for us even when we don't know what to pray (Romans 8:26), which is why it's crucial to pray in the Spirit.

If you recall, in During the Storm, I stressed the importance of not just praying, but also praying in the Spirit. When we pray in the Spirit we cover ourselves outside of our own intellect. I've always prayed in the Spirit so that Holy Spirit can pray on my behalf through the tongues. In addition to 1) praying from my own intellect, and 2) praying in the Spirit, I regularly inquire of the Lord, "What should I be praying?" A lot of times, we waste times in prayer when we can simply ask God what we should be praying for. That might sound strange, but the scripture says that He knows all and He knows what we have need for. If that's the case, why not ask God, "What do you want me to pray? "For whom do you want me to pray?" This practice allows me to pray the perfect will of God.

After going through each area, dissecting and examining the attack from various ways and finally discovering that this attack was from the enemy, I needed to know what to do — as it relates to my love walk, and if there were any bitterness, lack of forgiveness, or strife. When we are under an attack from the enemy, it can come from one of those avenues. In 1 Peter when the bible tells us to be sober and vigilant, because our adversary the enemy walks to and fro seeking whom he may devour, it's alerting us that in line with his job description, after an assignment from the pit of hell has come into our lives or homes, Satan will discover different things about us based on doors that we may have opened. Relative to spiritual matters, we need to be on our game. It's dangerous to walk around in bitterness. We need to stay out of offense and stay out of strife. Personally, I know someone right now whose healing is being blocked because of offense. In the scriptures, we see where John the Baptist literally got his head in a very bad place, on a silver platter, simply put. While he was in prison, he became offended that Jesus didn't get him out. He sent his disciples out to ask Jesus if he was the One or should they look for another. John's disciples and John himself knew who Jesus was, and that comment was based on offense and strife. Who knows what Jesus might have done had John not fallen into offense, but he did, and the offense that succumbed him took his head off his shoulders. In response to John's disciples, Jesus told them, "Blessed are those who are not offended by me." Obviously, people who fall into offense (like John the Baptist) block blessings and succumb to demonic attacks.

The scripture says "having done all… then stand." The problem I've discovered in most cases when people are defeated or lose out on the promises of God is that they try to stand, without first having done all. It says, "after having done all," meaning AFTERWARDS... after you've done all that you can do you will have the ability to stand. There's an account in the bible when someone tried to present a gift in the offering, and Jesus said, 'Go back and correct that thing with your brother and then come back and give your offering.' There are a lot of things that could be standing in the way of your healing or opening the door to poverty or defeat—you have to do your part.

No weapon formed against you shall prosper,

And every tongue which rises against you in judgment

You shall condemn.

This is the heritage of the servants of the Lord,

And their righteousness is from Me,"

Says the Lord

Isaiah 54:17

The bible does not say that weapons would not be formed, but instead, we see that weapons that are formed that will not prosper. I had to take the time to investigate the storm enough to find out if this was in fact a weapon from Satan. I felt confident that it was and yet through the Word, I knew that it would not conquer me.

CHAPTER 4:
STORMS FROM THE WORLD

I have told you all this so that you may have peace in me.

Here on earth you will have many trials and sorrows.

But take heart, because I have overcome the world.

John 16:33

Satan gets blamed for far too much because we don't know where attacks come from. This is why after your storm it is crucial for you to determine the root of the disruption. Did the enemy really send this storm or could it perhaps be one sent from the world? If we bind the devil and cast out demons when we face storms that stem from the world, we will not be effective. Instead, when these storms occur, we must confess the word, stand, and remain in peace. After these storms, we can remain in authority if we remain in the word, and if we STAND.

One of the most challenging jobs to do as a pastor is to console fathers, mothers, sisters, and brothers when they have just lost a loved one. There are not many words to say, and often, there are no worldly explanations for the types of crises believers endure… Think about the random car accident, the critical fall or mistake that leads to injury. The scripture states that in this world, there will be tribulation, but we are instructed to be of good cheer, for Jesus has overcome the world. Because we are in Christ, we too have overcome the storms of this world.

Storms from the world are different from storms sent by Satan, and they require a different strategy to fight them and to examine them. The attacks that we face in this world were put into motion at the point of the fall of Adam and Eve. Evil, death, destruction, pain, and imperfection have as equal right to work throughout our world as goodness and blessings. It's important to understand, prepare, and discern the storms that enter your life by virtue of you living in this world. These are the storms that did not result from anything that you or any of us have done. They were also not released by Satan, yet instead, they are storms that have manifested because we're living on earth. This is sort of like car accidents. They shouldn't happen, but they often do and they interrupt any given day, and no one in particular may be at fault. As licensed drivers on a road with hundreds and thousands of other cars, we take risks each day when we get on the road. We risk the possibility of encountering a storm sent by the world. We never know what may happen when we enter that car and begin driving. We cannot control the other drivers, the pace and rate of traffic, how many other people will be driving, and often we cannot control the accidents and fender benders that arise as a result. I was driving home one day from church and literally watched a young lady take her last breath as a result of another driver reaching for chicken. The other driver is alive and well, while this young lady is dead and her loved ones are left with her memory - from another's moment of neglect. Accidents can be just like storms sent from the world, and although we never know when one might arise, we still must prepare for them and repair after them.

PREPARE

Every licensed driver must attend driving school to learn techniques to prevent accidents and remain safe. We learn how to park, where to look for street instructions, and the difference between a red light for "stop" and a green light telling us to "go." We prepare by taking precautions. These steps are just like the pre-storm strategies in Before The Storm the actions we have taken prior to accidents or storms enabling us to remain safe and secure during. For instance, we are to anticipate car accidents by wearing seatbelts, adhering to speed limits and being cautious and aware of what's around us.

REPAIR

When there are accidents on the road, both drivers immediately assess the damage. Then, they seek support from police offers and insurance agents in order to set the repair process in motion. Now, let's just say that there's a town with a traffic circle and there are always accidents around and inside of that circle. At some point, elected officials will likely analyze and determine that more precautions or additional construction or repairs need to occur within that circle to prevent future accidents.

Driving school prepares us for the road before accidents occur. Experience behind the wheel teaches us how to become more savvy drivers to avoid accidents. Analyzing the causes of car accidents afterwards helps to circumvent future issues. This is the role your spiritual regiment plays as it relates to storms. Our pre-storm strategies in Before The Storm prepare us to take the road and endure hard times, and during the storm, with experience working our faith we become strong enough to stand. Your post-storm analysis will sharpen and refine you and often equip you to circumvent the same types of storms in the future. You wouldn't continue taking the same route with the faulty traffic circle if you didn't have to right? When attacks arise from the world, in some cases, a post-examination can reveal a different way of doing things and extra precautions that are needed.

Storms from the world may not always appear as some major catastrophe or loss either. Think about the times when you bump your big toe on the edge of furniture, by virtue of having furniture and having a big toe. Bumping your toe had nothing to do with Satan; it instead had everything to do with you being in the same place and space as furniture and not realizing that you were about to bump into it. This can reveal to you the need to pay closer attention to your surroundings. Other storms sent by the world, such as the car accident for instance may not have been your fault but because of your position in Christ you are still victorious—meaning, the storm does not need to defeat you or steal your peace. It doesn't even have to remain. As a joint heir in Christ, you have the power to seek God through prayer and ask Him how to be victorious in all areas. In the after-effect of these storms, you can experience peace in and take authority over them by confessing what the word says. Although the world sends us unpredictable storms, Jesus assures us in John 16:33 that we can take peace in Him because He has overcome the world.

CHAPTER 5:
SELF-INFLICTED STORMS

I don't really understand myself, for I want to do what is right,

but I don't do it. Instead, I do what I hate. But if I know that what

I am doing is wrong, this shows that I agree that the law is good.

So I am not the one doing wrong; it is sin living in me that does

it.

And I know that nothing good lives in me, that is, in my sinful

nature. I want to do what is right, but I can't. I want to do what

is good, but I don't. I don't want to do what is wrong, but I do it

anyway. But if I do what I don't want to do, I am not really the

one doing wrong; it is sin living in me that does it.

I have discovered this principle of life—that when I want to do what is right, I inevitably do what is wrong. I love God's law with all my heart But there is another power within me that is at war with my mind. This power makes me a slave to the sin that is still within me. Oh, what a miserable person I am! Who will free me from this life that is dominated by sin and death? Thank God! The answer is in Jesus Christ our Lord. So you see how it is: In my mind I really want to obey God's law, but because of my sinful nature I am a slave to sin.

Romans 7:15-25

Self-inflicted storms stem from our flesh. At the point of salvation, we received a new, perfect spirit man. However, we make decisions based on the soul, which is comprised of the mind, will, and emotions. The soul leans toward our fleshly desires until we learn to crucify the flesh and get the soul aligned with the spirit. In the passage above, the Apostle Paul was grappling with a fight that every believer deals with between the flesh and the spirit. Because the soul makes the decisions that ultimately affect the flesh, our goal as believers is to feed our spirit so that our natural (soul) desires become things aligned with the will of God.

Storms that we create for ourselves often arise when we pursue a thing to please our flesh, despite what the Spirit wants. Every person has a sinful nature and a desire to do what pleases the flesh, which is why the Apostle Paul instructed us to put to death the deeds of our sinful nature. Often, when we talk about "the flesh," as it relates to sin, the connotation cues thoughts about sex, greed, lust, and lying. However, self-inflicted storms (from the flesh) can be subtle in nature and they may seem less dangerous with limited consequences, but that is not always the case. The smallest mistakes or mishaps can erupt into major storms.

I loved to play basketball very much. One day, not too long ago, I truly was looking forward to a game of basketball all day. After ministering and doing everything else I had to do for the day, it was time to relax, but I really wanted to play ball. So, I dressed and went out to the court. I was already worn out, and right before I went outside, I heard Holy Spirit warn me not to go. However, because I wanted to play so badly, I brushed it off and dismissed His voice. So I went on the court and was playing ball. I went up to dunk the ball, came down and broke my leg right there on the spot. That was the last time I ever dunked a basketball, and I am the one to blame. Afterwards, all I could do is deal with the repercussions. I had received the warning and the Spirit alerted me not to play, but I did it anyway. I went through weeks of recovery and now I am no longer able to play ball like before.

We do a lot of things that we know we should not be doing. We know the risks, receive the warnings, and yet we allow our fleshly desires to lead and we go against our better judgement. These are self-inflicted attacks. These come in many different forms and can affect any area of our lives including, finances, health, relationships, spirituality—you name it. Often, these storms or attacks arise from doing something we knew that we should not have been doing—the result is being thrust into storms. It's just like a bank robber or someone else who commits a crime, or a person who knowingly overeats, or that person who eats what they are allergic to just because it tastes good. Some things are self-inflicted. God tells us not to do one thing, but we do it anyway. This causes some unnecessary drama because of the law of sowing and reaping. The mishaps come from disobedience and the willful desires to do whatever it is that we have willed to do. You can probably recall a time when you did something you had no business doing or you didn't do something that you should have been doing. When we go against the Believer's Instructions Before Leaving Earth (BIBLE) wisdom, we open ourselves up to self-inflicted storms and attacks.

Consider the various types of financial storms and how these types of storms may appear from various perspectives (storms from the enemy, the world, and self-inflicted). In the early 2000s there was a major scandal surrounding the Enron Corporation, which was a Houston-based energy company. The leaders of that company were found to have hid (or embezzled) billions of dollars, and their stock plummeted from over $90 per share to less than $1. Several leaders of that company were found guilty of various charges and were sentenced to prison. This was the largest corporate bankruptcy in the history of America. It has become synonymous with corporate greed and The Wall Street scandal. There were many people affected by this scandal who had nothing to do with it. Now, while the storm that Enron leaders experienced after they were caught (imprisonment, embarrassment, loss, and scandal) was self-inflicted due to selfish ambitions and greed, there were also many unsuspecting people caught in the storm. Those victims experienced a storm orchestrated by the enemy and sent from the pit of hell. The enemy is the author of lies, deception, and manipulation. His job description is to kill, steal, and destroy. The leaders involved in this scandal were operating according to principles from the kingdom of darkness and they became conduits of Satan's agenda to steal finances and destroy the lives and businesses of those involved. The countless families who suffered as a result of this level of greed were caught in the evil path of this storm that arose from the pit of hell. Here we saw an example of free-will that turned into greed and had a domino effect on America's financial landscape.

A financial attack from the world could include a wave of unexpected layoffs on the job leading to many unemployed people. This storm may not stem from the enemy nor be caused by a particular person. However, the nature of business and the changing climate of business or industry can lead to this type of financial storm, which can have a domino effect for those involved. This is an example of a financial storm from the world.

Now, imagine a person losing his or her job and facing a month full of bills and no money in the bank. While this person had been earning more than enough for years prior to being laid-off, instead of saving, they shopped excessively, dined out, and spent frivolous money on entertainment and worldly possessions. This person was operating against biblical principles. Over and over the bible instructs us to be prudent and it clarifies that prudence is a heavenly virtue deposited to those in Christ.

The prudent sees danger and hides himself, but the simple

go on and suffer for it.Proverbs 22:3

"Then the kingdom of heaven will be like ten virgins who

took their lamps and went to meet the bridegroom. Five of

them were foolish, and five were wise. For when the foolish

took their lamps, they took no oil with them, but the wise

took flasks of oil with their lamps...

Matthew 25:1-15

The way of a fool is right in his own eyes, but a wise man

listens to advice. The vexation of a fool is known at once,

but the prudent ignores an insult.

Proverbs 12:15

I, wisdom, dwell with prudence, and I find knowledge and

discretion.

Proverbs 8:12

In everything the prudent acts with knowledge, but a fool

flaunts his folly.

Proverbs 13:16

Prudence means acting or showing care or thought for the future. It is marked by wisdom and judiciousness. Many people are careless with their income and lives. Those who do not live by any plan or budget, those who do not save and tithe with their earnings and have specific assignments for their finances are not behaving in wisdom. These individuals are compulsive in their spending and when something arises after there has been improper financial management, these individuals end up in a jam. They did not expect an unexpected bill, loss of income, or car troubles, so they have created financial crises for themselves. Satan did not send those storms and neither did the world. God provides us opportunity and free will and many people create financial crises simply because they have activated a free will to spend as they please. Christian financial guru Dave Ramsey has a financial program called Financial Peace University, based on biblical principles. This program helps its students develop a mindset and plan to build wealth through implementing what he calls five "baby steps." I appreciate this program, because the first baby step for its students is to establish an emergency fund that includes a minimum of $1,000 in a savings account. He instructs students to continue saving until the account grows to at least six months' worth of living expenses. This type of financial prudence will help believers avoid financial related, self-inflicted storms.

LAW OF SOWING AND REAPING

Many people bring storms on themselves and others experience storms because they break the law of sowing and reaping. The Word is very clear; Galatians 6:7: Do not be deceived: God cannot be mocked. A man reaps what he sows. The law of sowing and reaping is vitally critical in the storm strategies, because storms can often be avoided. "For a good tree does not bear bad fruit, nor does a bad tree bear good fruit. A tree is identified by its fruit. For every tree is known by its own fruit. For men do not gather figs from thorns, nor do they gather grapes from a bramble bush." (Luke 6:43-44). This means that if one sows poor financial management, he or she will reap the repercussions in the form of financial attacks. If one sows poor health, this person will reap the fruit of that in the form health disparities or illness. Many people get caught up as it pertains to health attacks, because the fruit of poor health may take years to sprout. If a doctor instructs a man not to eat sodium or to keep certain types of food from his diet and the man continues to eat salty, unhealthy foods, the fruit of that behavior will likely be high blood pressure and heart issues.

Self-inflicted storms may also arise from relationships that had warning signs written all over them. Family members and friends may have warned against a certain relationship, yet a person will continue to invest time and resources and eventually something bad happens such as domestic violence or betrayal. While these incidents are unfortunate, and I am not giving anyone a pass on violent or immoral actions, each person has choices and often there are warnings and indicators—such as the Holy Spirit check—or warnings from loved ones that people ignore because of their own will. Storms of this manner are self-inflicted and often avoidable. My prayer is that you will begin to dissect your storms with great scrutiny and precision so that you can see them from the various angles. This will cause you to grow more alert, discerning, prudent, and wise.

While many self-inflicted storms arise from disobedience (such as my Holy Spirit basketball check) and selfish desires or temptation from the enemy (such as the Enron scandal); self-inflicted storms may also arise from human error and mistakes. Myles Munroe was one of the greatest pastors and theologians of our age, and he is with Jesus today because of a human-error. He did nothing wrong, but he died in a plane crash that investigations later revealed was caused because his plane was not supposed to be flying from the particular airport where the flight originated at the time, yet the officials chose to fly anyway. The Federal Aviation Administration investigates the scenes of air crashes afterwards, and many of these cases have been attributed to human error.

Self-inflicted attacks are preventable, and those that stem from human error are often a result of a disobedience, lack of focus, or arrogance/pride.

In relation to this topic, I must bring up the topic of grace. There have been some phenomenal teachings on the grace of God and the new covenant of grace that we have with God as a result of Jesus' work on the cross. However, in some cases, this message has been twisted to make believers think they have a pass to do and live how they want without any repercussions and consequences, simply because they are forgiven and their salvation cannot be taken away. While it may be true that God forgives and once we are saved, everlasting life is guaranteed, the law of sowing and reaping tells us that there are still consequences on earth. The Apostle Paul puts it like this, "Whoever sows to please their flesh, from the flesh will reap destruction; whoever sows to please the

Spirit, from the Spirit will reap eternal life," (Galatians 6:8).

By virtue of the law of sowing a reaping, whatever a man sows, and I repeat, whatever a man or woman sows, he or she will reap. That's why I'm writing this book. If I can share my story and thinking about what I did or did not do, perhaps it can circumvent the attack on your lives. Even as I'm writing, I am praying for you, that you will cover all areas to the best of your abilities.

It is far time that we take our walk with God seriously. Storms that stem from sin are preventable if we remove the sin. Yes, there are some things that we do or overlook and they are unintentional. Many times, however, believers are not holding this type of mirror to themselves and some would rather hide sin or ignore character issues that cause self-inflicted storms. The scripture says he who hides his sin will not prosper, but the one who confesses and renounces them obtains mercy (Proverbs 28:13). Mercy is the act of showing compassion or forbearance to an offender. When God gives mercy after we have sinned and caused a self-inflicted attack, we are not receiving the full blown aftermath/punishment that our actions warrant. It's just like a serial killer who is sentenced to life in prison verses the death penalty; or the promiscuous young adult who never contracts HIV or AIDS.

When you identify a self-inflicted storm, you want to first

confess and renounce any sins that you've committed that have left you exposed. If the storm was unintentional or due to ignorance or error, pray for the Holy Spirit to lead and guide you to truth. If you are unsure of what has happened to cause your storm, if you ask Holy Spirit to bring some back to your remembrance, He has promised that He will do just that.

As you equip yourself for your next storm, become sharper, more committed and more obedient so that you aren't the cause of your own evil day. With focus, prayer, and righteous living, many of the self-inflicted storms you experience will cease.

PRAYER TO COVER SELF-INFLICTED STORMS:

Dear Father,

I repent of my sins, the disobedience, lack of focus, pride, evil desires, lust, and carelessness that caused any self-inflicted storms. Lord, I plead the blood of Jesus over my mind, body, and soul, and I re-commit myself to your will for my life. Lord, please release your ministering angels to protect and guard me against demonic attacks and temptations.

Thank you for deliverance and discernment.

In Jesus' name, Amen.

CHAPTER 6:
FRUIT FROM THE STORM

But Joseph said to them, "Don't be afraid. Am I in the

place of God?

You intended to harm me, but God intended it for good to

accomplish what is now being done, the saving of many

lives.

Genesis 50:19-20

As we've established, the storm you encountered was meant to take you out. The next storm that you encounter will be designed to take you out. That knowledge should not make you afraid, nor will you back down. The point of The Storm Series is to equip you to circumvent storms, stand in storms, and overcome and emerge victorious from storms. In the case that you are not able to circumvent them, you will be strong enough to stand.

Therefore put on the full armor of God, so that when the

day of evil comes, you may be able to stand your ground,

and after you have done everything, to stand.

Ephesians 6:13

After you have done everything Before The Storm, you stand. You stand During The Storm with the full armor of God.

Stand firm then, with the belt of truth buckled around your

waist, with the breastplate of righteousness in place, and

with your feet fitted with the readiness that comes from the

gospel of peace. In addition to all this, take up the shield of

faith, with which you can extinguish all the flaming arrows

of the evil one. Take the helmet of salvation and the sword

of the Spirit, which is the word of God.

Ephesians 6:14-17

The bible tells us what to do. If you remain steadfast in your faith—meaning you are unwavering, not willing to back down, you will survive. There is nothing to fear about the attacks you have and will experience.

GOOD TREE, GOOD FRUIT

At the time of me writing this book, it is hurricane season. Thus far, in the past month or so, Hurricane Harvey has uprooted many people and businesses in Texas and most recently Hurricane Irma has rocked the core of Puerto Rico, leaving that island without electricity, medicine for hospital patients, food and basic survival necessities. I've been perplexed as to the role that believers had and are playing to prevent the types of disasters we are seeing in our country—both "natural," and pure evil (such as violence and mass shootings). I am convinced that we are not on our job. There is a prophet who prophesied a major storm to hit Houston months before Harvey actually arrived. That prophet instructed us to pray—pray without ceasing as we should be doing anyway per our instructions from 1 Thessalonians 5:17. I am convinced that many Christians have failed to pray against these types of storms. I'm convinced that we have stepped off of our posts. I believe that we allow, and in some cases, invite many of these governmental, natural, social, economic, and relational storms by failing to pray and failing to speak against these storms.

If someone walked into your house right now and told you that you were a no good loser and that you were going to be ruined in the upcoming days or weeks, would you allow that? Would you accept it? No, I seriously doubt it. You'd ask that person to be quiet and get out of your house. Perhaps as a Christian, you would pray for that person. My point is that you would not accept those types of word curses in your life. Sad thing is that many believers accept that type of behavior from the enemy… or the world, or through their own actions and words, themselves. The storms have been allowed, welcomed, and perpetuated because in many cases, prayer is lacking. We must learn how to pray and speak against those storms. Reject, rebuke and pray against them. In Appendix 1 at the end of this book there are confessions and scripture to strengthen you as you begin to speak against the storms that arise in your life. The very fruit from your storm is directly related to how and what you pray during your storm.

The Old Testament book of 1 Samuel documents Israel's transition from a theocracy (a nation ruled by God) to a monarchy (one ruled by a king). Samuel was the last judge of Israel and the prophet that God used to anoint the first two kings—King Saul and King David. While Samuel was the Lord's trusted servant and a mighty man of God, the circumstances surrounding his birth can be described as hopeless and desperate. See, Samuel's mother Hannah was barren—and it looked like she had no possibility of having any children. She was desperate and on top of that, her husband had a side chick— (well, not exactly)—he had a second wife who behaved like a side chick. She chastised Hannah because she (the side chick-wife) was able to have children and Hannah could not. She desperately wanted to have at least one child. The bible says in 1 Samuel 1:6-7, "Because the Lord had closed Hannah's womb, her rival kept provoking her in order to irritate her. This went on year after year. Whenever Hannah went up to the house of the Lord, her rival provoked her till she wept and would not eat." As you can see, Hannah had it bad. So what did she do? She prayed. She put her situation on the altar. During her life's greatest storm—mental anguish, desperation, depression, bullying, hopelessness, and barrenness—she devoted herself to praying for that thing which she desired. And she believed that God would provide it too. Verses 10-11 read, "In her deep anguish Hannah prayed to the Lord, weeping bitterly. And she made a vow, saying, "Lord Almighty, if you will only look on your servant's misery and remember me, and not forget your servant but give her a son, then I will give him to the Lord for all the days of his life, and no razor will ever be used on his head." She prayed. The prophet Samuel was fruit from her lifestyle of prayer. After him, God continued to respond to Hannah's prayers with three more sons and two daughters.

That's called fruit from the storm.

A good tree cannot bear bad fruit, nor can a bad tree bear

good fruit. Every tree that does not bear good fruit is cut

down and thrown into the fire. Therefore by their fruits you

will know them.

Matthew 7:18-20

After you experience something life-altering, you will never be the same, and you aren't designed to be. Although it shouldn't take storms in life to make you better, you should naturally draw closer to God. You should be praying more. Your prayer life and the other seeds that you've planted have fruit attached to them. You will reap what you sow, including in prayer.

GOD'S BIG BUT

Let's look at another example. In the book of Genesis, we see the age-old battle of good against evil play out in many ways. There is deception, theft, kidnapping, adultery, fornication, murder, rape and so forth. For the Word of God to begin with such vivid and clear narratives about how humankind dealt with storms and trials, there are important lessons and a message here. God wants us to know and see that from the beginning since the fall of Adam and Eve, the human species has dealt with tough and hard times—and yet, He has remained faithful. There are many lessons to learn about storms from this first book of the bible from the lives of Adam and Eve; Cain and Abel, Isaac and Ishmael, and Joseph.

Joseph was a young dreamer who knew as a young man that he would ultimately rule over his brothers. Upon hearing this dream interpretation, of course the brothers were jealous of Joseph and they threw him in a pit and faked his death. Joseph faced storm after storm starting with that incident. The devil designed his doom's day many times, BUT we see that God never left him. Joseph was covered the entire time. The favor on the life of a believer does not lift or dissipate just because he or she is in a bad way like Joseph. God keeps us during the storm and prepares us for the fruit that will come forth after.

After Joseph arose victoriously from the series of life storms that stemmed from his jealous brothers throwing him in a pit and selling him into slavery, he was finally reunited with his family. His brothers thought that he would want to get revenge on them for causing so much pain in his life. However, Joseph realized the favor on his life—and even throughout his darkest times, God was there with him. Joseph's story embodies the very mind, heart and promises of God. He did indeed rule over his brothers but it was in love. He provided for them, even after burying his father. God's promises are true and so are life's storms. A storm cannot cancel a promise. When you get through the storm, there will be fruit. Often, after we successfully make it through a storm, we have an assignment and a bigger territory—just as Joseph did.

The Lord says to my lord:

"Sit at my right hand

until I make your enemies

a footstool for your feet."

Psalm 110:1

Being transparent, it was so unfortunate and sometimes even heart wrenching to see some of my brothers and sisters in the Body of Christ attacking me during the storm that was designed to kill me. Just like Joseph, I set myself to love them in spite of their harsh treatment and unkind words. Always be bigger than the attack of the enemy, and as he turns up the volume - you turn up your love walk!

The Psalmist David documented a promise from God that

we see play out throughout the ages—redemption and recovery. While I do not prescribe to the thought that our storms are sent by God, we know that as a result of God's promises to us, He has the power and the desire to make our storms transform into blessings for His kingdom. This is the spirit of Romans 8:28, "And we know that all things work together for good to those who love God, to those who are the called according to His purpose." The very fact that you are reading this book is an example of that.

Not only did I regain my health, but my family and I came out of the storm with fruit. For starters, and most importantly, we have won souls to Christ and many people have received Jesus. In addition to that, some of those individuals even became partners with us in ministry. The head man who was at the rehabilitation facility is now the health and wellness director at my church. Prior to meeting DeeDee and I, he was not attending church. Not only that, but my respiratory therapist is now also a partner of the ministry as well. It's so powerful to see what had been a death threat for me become a promise of life for others.

We have to always take a redress. After the storm is over, we have to come back and bring everything into its proper prospective, just like Joseph did. In a worldly view, he had every right to be mad and angry at his brothers, but he chose to operate by God's principals instead. This is important, because it ties back to a pre-storm strategy of "Fail Not to Forgive." Joseph could not live in non-forgiveness towards his brothers and expect the full blessings and promises for his life to manifest. Remember that your fruit will be determined by the seeds you plant. So you cannot sow seeds of non-forgiveness and anger and expect fruit of peace and joy.

This is the stage when you can gain a new perspective on your storm. It is amazing how a situation can appear to be one thing, but after you look at it, you can redress it and come out thanking God even more. Going through the storm caused me to begin to look at all the situations in my life as circumstances that provided a benefit to me and others. Although it was designed to kill me, it helped make me. Again, I am not subscribing to theology that says, "God sent this storm or the storm happened to make me stronger," because trials don't come to make us strong, they come to kill us. However, when we survive them, we can learn many things and grow as a result. Upon my return to ministry, everyone on the staff and many of our church partners at Spirit of Faith wore shirts that read, "We Win." I've come to realize that as believers, we don't ever have to lose. I say that sometimes you win and sometimes you learn. I heard that somewhere and it's been a part of my thinking ever since.

In hindsight, I can't tell you the amount of people that this storm has helped. When we redressed this storm, we looked back and saw that God received all of the glory. I don't believe anyone has to go through anything to become who and what they are. I believe that you can be taught by the Word of God and be all that God calls you to be. Jesus never went through any marital problems, but he could counsel on marriage. He never experienced any sickness at all except what was put on him at the very end. He grew and learned the Word by sitting at God's feet and hearing from God. Hebrews 5:7-8 reads, "During the days of Jesus' earthly life, He offered up prayers and petitions with loud cries and tears to the One who could save Him from death, and He was heard because of His reverence. Although He was a Son, He learned obedience from what He suffered." It wasn't the suffering that was the teacher. The teacher had already taught the student, and He (Jesus) learned obedience and saw that it works through the suffering that he went through. If we approach that scripture from the standpoint that suffering teaches us obedience and makes us who we are supposed to be, it's equivalent to taking a child's hand and putting it over a flaming stove. We don't do that. We don't subject them to suffering second or third degree burns and then say, "Now, you see this stove will burn you, so never put your hand over the flame again." Instead, we show them the stove. We let them know it is hot so that they do not have to be burned in order to learn the lesson. I think a big part of the body of Christ thinks that there must be some burn in order for them to learn the lesson. That's not true, but once we are burned, we learn that the stove is hot and that the principles we were taught actually work. The Word works, and I'd take that over the storm any day.

Here's a bit of homework, I want you to look at the word suffer in the Hebrew and Greek to see for yourself what suffering actually meant in Hebrew 5:8.

TESTIMONIES

I was sitting in a meeting once with Dr. Price (big shout out to him), and several of the guys in the meeting were sharing their testimonies. It was interesting to be sitting right next to him and hearing him reply and respond to the stories that were being shared. One guy spoke up, and his story was truly profound. God had brought him out of various storms, and many of them were self-inflicted. Dr. Price was speaking to me personally, and in response to this one particular testimony, he said,

"That guy has been through some things."

And I said, "Yes sir he has."

"That sounds so dramatic and so interesting," he began. "I would love to have one of those testimonies where the Lord had delivered me from something like that…" Then, Dr. Price paused as if to make sure that he would carefully articulate what he was about to share. He continued, "But when you think about it, who has the better testimony? The one who went through something terrible who had to learn the Word through that testimony or the one who learned the Word and didn't have to go through that bad thing that gave them the testimony?" This conversation made me think if we took the Word of God, worked the Word in our lives, and built ourselves up, we could circumvent many storms. The bible promises to show us things to come. We will be so prepared when we already see storms coming, just by knowing the Word. Then, we wouldn't have to suffer so much.

Let's go back to before the storm for a moment. When the meteorologist says a storm is coming, we board up windows, stock up on supplies, and purchase back-up generators. We are ready and prepared. We have extra food, water, batteries, gas in the car, snow boots, shovels—you name it. The meteorologist provides us with the probability rate of the storm in terms of percentages—40%

chance of snowfall or 20% chance of rain. We also know the speed and whereabouts of certain storms such as tornadoes and hurricanes.

Sometimes, these storms actually come to our geographic regions and sometimes they don't. However, regardless of what the storm does, we are STILL prepared. If the storm does not come, it cannot cause any damage whatsoever. The point is that we are already prepared. After you have been through something, you learn a lot about how not to have to face it again. I think that's the whole intent that Jesus wanted us to get through many of His teachings. Jesus was not saying, go stick your hand in the fire so you can learn this lesson about how not to get burned. He taught the truth and told us that if we follow His instructions, we would get to where we need to go. One of the best fruit from storms is additional wisdom and ability to avoid storms in the future.

STRENGTHENING OTHERS

After a storm, you will be called and expected by God to uplift others. You will also be equip to do so. Often, you will see that those who've survived a thing have the ability and knowledge (and Holy Spirit power) to minister to others who are going through the same circumstance. The scripture is clear about coming out and strengthening your "brothers."

During the last supper, the disciples were engaged in a fickle and prideful dispute about who among them were the greatest. I imagine that Peter, being the boldest and most courageous one had a lot to say about this matter. He was the first disciple who received the revelation that Jesus was the Messiah. He was also the one who had walked on water. Although the bible doesn't say, he probably reminded his friends about all that he had done and perhaps he boasted that he was the greatest of the twelve disciples. I mention that point because pride is an entryway to attacks from the enemy; pride comes before destruction and a haughty spirit before a fall (Proverbs 16:18). Immediately after this argument, in his gospel, Luke documents Jesus' warning to Peter of an approaching storm.

And the Lord said,[c] "Simon, Simon! Indeed, Satan has asked for you, that he may sift you as wheat. But I have prayed for you, that your faith should not fail; and when you have returned to Me, strengthen your brethren."

Luke 22:31-32

Peter indeed went on to face one of the toughest moments

of his life as a disciple. His teacher, the Messiah was on His way to death, and just as He said, Peter denied that he even knew Jesus—three times. Satan sifted him; Peter's fear of persecution caused him to fall out faith. The enemy had a temporary win. Jesus was on the cross about to die. Next in line, Peter, had denied even knowing Jesus; another one, Judas, had been an accomplice to Jesus' murder… Indeed, Satan must have thought he won. The disciples were scared and fearful and with them dropping off like flies, there was no way that Jesus' message would spread. However, even during his final moments—as the disciples immaturely bickered about who was better—and hours before his death—knowing that he'd hang up there alone, Jesus gave Peter instructions. He reassured His disciple that Hey, I know what's about to happen to you. You're going to bail out on me, but even still—I forgive you. I have faith in your faith! I know what's in you, and my promise to you of building the church with you at the forefront still stands. When you come back to my kingdom, you have work to do. Strengthen your brothers! Jesus gave Peter a pep talk that shed light on a biblical principle that Jesus wants us to follow. After we are redeemed, we must help others. Peter probably couldn't fully grasp the full meaning of what Jesus had said until after Jesus died and resurrected.

Just as Jesus loved Peter through His storm, he does the same for us even today. We are forever forgiven for our mishaps, trip-ups, for falling to temptation and losing our way. Peter did in fact take Jesus' instructions literally and went on to preach the sermon at the greatest revival in the history of the world—Pentecost—when believers received the gift of speaking in tongues, received Jesus and worshipped like never before. Up until the Apostle Paul hit the scene and was charged with spreading the gospel to the gentiles, Peter was the leader—the aftermath of his storm laid the important foundations of our faith.

CHAPTER 7:
STORM SURVIVORS

Then Job replied to the Lord:

"I know that you can do all things;

no purpose of yours can be thwarted.

You asked, 'Who is this that obscures my plans without

knowledge?'

Surely I spoke of things I did not understand,

things too wonderful for me to know.

"You said, 'Listen now, and I will speak;

I will question you,

and you shall answer me.'

My ears had heard of you

but now my eyes have seen you.

Therefore I despise myself

and repent in dust and ashes."

Epilogue

After the Lord had said these things to Job, he said to

Eliphaz the Temanite, "I am angry with you and your

two friends, because you have not spoken the truth about

me, as my servant Job has. So now take seven bulls and

seven rams and go to my servant Job and sacrifice a

burnt offering for yourselves. My servant Job will pray

for you, and I will accept his prayer and not deal with

you according to your folly. You have not spoken the truth

about me, as my servant Job has." So Eliphaz the Temanite,

Bildad the Shuhite and Zophar the Naamathite did what the

Lord told them; and the Lord accepted Job's prayer.

After Job had prayed for his friends, the Lord restored his

fortunes and gave him twice as much as he had before.

Job 42:1-10

If you will notice, when Job went through his storm, he had friends who would not stand with him. They accused him for the trouble that he went through and they even suggested that he curse God and die. Thank God Job never paid any attention to them or his wife and God gave him double for the trouble that he went through because he maintained his course throughout his storm. Job also repented for his own moments of wavering faith, and he prayed for his friends. This combination of repentance and prayer proved his faithfulness, and he ended up prospering and experiencing greater wealth and good fortune. It's going to take the Spirit of the living God and the knowledge of the living God, and His word by the power of the Spirit, to be able to walk through and help others on the other end. We don't know whether or not those friendships survived the storm, but had I been Job, after coming out of the storm I would have literally continued with some of those people of my team to assist them like Joseph and his brothers; maybe all of them.

WHERE ARE YOUR STORM SURVIVORS?

There will be people who supposedly had your back before a storm but disappeared once you found yourself going through. After you go through the process of examining the storm, you must reconsider your team. Everyone needs people on their team who cares about their dream. During my storm, there were people in my life who never called and checked on us—people who I don't even think prayed for us. And as I've mentioned before, unfortunately, some with ulterior motives, who thought I was dead or dying attempted to get closer to my wife DeeDee because of all of the material things that I possessed. They were positioning themselves to become beneficiaries of those things, but they didn't really care about what we were going through. You have to determine who is who as well as keep your heart right about these people. Even when you determine that some people mean you no well, you should not grow angry or hold any grudges. It is what it is. As a survivor of something of this magnitude, you have no time to waste being angry or upset about what someone did or didn't do. Just be glad that the fire you went through served as a refining process to get rid of the excess people in your life.

After the storm, DeeDee and I sat down and discussed people who we could always call. It was a very real conversation, because we had to compare notes. I was in a hospital for quite some time, while she and my brother and associate pastor took care of the ministry. I had to trust and allow the Holy Spirit to guide us. We discussed whom we could call if something was to happen to either of us ever again—who could pray, who could step into positions of leadership, who could we trust and with what areas? It is vitally important that you evaluate the people who were in your life before the storm. Did they stand the test of being in it?

Are they storm survivors? We discussed getting your team in order in our pre-storm strategies in Before The Storm, but at the same time, you can evaluate, whether the people who were in your life before the storm stood throughout the storm or did they abandon you?

In our post-storm explorations, there were some people who we discovered that although we love them very dearly, we would never want them to be a part of our inner squad or team again if God forbid something of this magnitude ever happens. Know your go-to people. Don't put this process off another day. I've been forewarning you throughout this series that there will be another evil day, and you never know when that will be. Unfortunately, many people must discover these lessons the hard way. They have people around that they think they can count on only to find out they are not reliable. This was the case with Job. When he lost everything he thought that he had friends and a wife who would have some kind of compassion and who could help him make sense of what he was dealing with. Unfortunately, it was exactly the opposite. These people made him feel worst.

Your "storm survivors" should consist of people who live by the word, walk by faith and strive to have a heart like Jesus. These are dependable and consistent people, those who can encourage and pray with you, take a load off of your back, bring sunlight in your life when your storm is closing in on you.

Everyone is different and not every person in your life will handle storms the same way—know their roles—but they should possess a level of faith that matches or often exceeds yours. After your storm, think back through the interactions that you've had with people in your circle and how they communicated with you during your storm. Seek the Lord for guidance and ask Him to reveal who should be close to you and who shouldn't.

No one is an island, so please don't take this as your cue to begin cutting everyone off or to be fickle with people who genuinely love and care for you just because they don't do what you want when you want. Get real and be an adult about this process. In the last chapter, we discussed the fruit from the storm. The people who survive your storm may become a part of your next season. If you are having trouble figuring out who is who, remember that as a believer, your purpose is to be building the kingdom of God. If the people who have been a part of your squad cannot help you do that, and vice versa, they are probably not designed to be in your inner squad. Just because they can't be apart of the inner circle doesn't mean that they can't be apart at all.

Another aspect of this entire conversation about survivors of the storm are the new people who entered your life as a result of your storm. God does His work on earth through His body of believers. Many times, the people who help us during the storm are not people that we know or have been closest with. Just like there were medical professionals who helped saved my life, whom I had not met prior to this storm, and are now in my life permanently, there may also be some people who were critical to your surviving. These are divine assignments in a way. Everyone has an assignment—be it a people group, geographic region or a niche or special interest. There are also people who may have been assigned to your life just to help you get through a storm—seasonal people. This is fine too. The point is that you should give it some thought. Do the right people have the proper access to you and your life? Have you overlooked potential covenant partnerships or destiny relationships because you've been distracted with people who do not belong? It's something to consider.

After the storm, your sphere of influence will change. It may seem to be diminishing at first because of a tendency to isolate oneself when going through difficult times—or because of your process of evaluating and eliminating people who did not stand with you during your storm. The ultimate result of your storm, however, will probably be a greater, more refined sphere of influence. The survivors of the storm will include people who've you met as a result of what has transpired in your life. Think of the divorcee who seeks support from others who have been through the same type of trial. Through groups at church, online forums, clubs for singles, and so forth, this person will meet a new tribe of people who share common interests—healing, recovery, and fellowship. Be open to the new direction in which God is moving you and the connections that you are establishing after the storm.

I am in a greater place today than I was prior to my storm. Just like Job, God has restored my family and I and we have prospered in every aspect of our lives. Although many people have been blessed by my story, I do not believe by any stretch of the imagination that this is something that I had to go through to know the power of God. God never intended for us to face some of the challenges we endure in life. Yes, the storm helped us attest to the goodness of God; it may have refined us, made us stronger, and produced fruit—but it was not necessary. I am thankful that my story can help us, and I thank God that I've partnered with God to put you in a position to storm proof your house before the next one comes to threaten your foundation.

Heavenly Father, Lord Almighty,

I thank you for your children who are reading this prayer right now.

Lord, I pray that their faith has been stirred up and activated, that they have gained a deeper knowledge of your word, and understanding of your ways. I pray that they continue to walk according your ways and that through wisdom, they will circumvent and discern the nature and originator of their storms. Lord, empower them to circumvent the unnecessary storms in their lives and stand firm in faith against those that they must endure. I pray for their protection, that they walk in love, and keep you lifted above everything and everyone else.

In Jesus' name,

Amen.

Appendix
SPEAK TO YOUR STORM

The power of the enemy has been broken by the blood of Jesus
Christ.

Satan has no authority.

Satan is defeated because of the Lord Jesus Christ.

I rebuke this storm and return it to sender in the name of Jesus
Christ.

As a citizen of the kingdom of heaven, I command this storm to
move in the name of Jesus.

I come against all attacks on my mind and thoughts that would
provoke me to sabotage

myself. I have complete control and I command my mind to align
with the Word of God.

I command all natural disasters and storm assigned to my region
and country to return to the where they originated and in the name
of the Lord Jesus Christ, I declare this storm ineffective.

Because God's children are human beings—made of flesh and blood—the Son also became flesh and blood. For only as a human being could he die, and only by dying could he break the power of the devil, who had the power of death.

Hebrews 2:14

For he has rescued us from the kingdom of darkness and transferred us into the Kingdom of his dear Son

Colossians 1:13

In this way, he disarmed the spiritual rulers and authorities. He shamed them publicly by his victory over them on the cross.

Colossians 2:1

And they have defeated him by the blood of the Lamb and by their testimony.

And they did not love their lives so much that they were afraid to die.

Revelation 12:11

ABOUT THE AUTHOR

Bold, compassionate, candid, relatable and kind; these are just some of the words that describe Mike Freeman.

A fourth generation pastor, Dr. Freeman continued his fore-fathers' legacies when he founded Spirit of Faith Christian Center (SOFCC). He believes his God-ordained assignment is to minister to the whole man - spirit, soul and body – by focusing on faith, family, finances and fellowship. Simply put - Pastor Freeman's heart is to teach people how to achieve God's best for their lives with simplicity and understanding

Founded in 1993, Spirit of Faith Christian Center is one of the fastest growing ministries in the nation. With three unique locations in Maryland, SOFCC has become home to both pastors

and parishioners. Dr. Freeman's profound understanding of the Word of God, coupled with his apparent love for people, have resulted in him being one of the most requested speakers in the body of Christ.

He and his wife, Deloris, (affectionately known as DeeDee), have created Marriage Made Easy, a ministry designed to share God's intent for marriage. Dr. Freeman also is the Chairman for, The Fellowship (Formally known as FICWFM), an internationally known minister's organization founded by Apostle Frederick K.C. Price.

The Freemans also share their teachings via Living by Faith, the ministry's television broadcast.

Dr. Freeman enjoys loving relationship with his wife, DeeDee, their three children - Brittney (husband-Kevin), Joshua, and Brelyn (husband-Tim), and five adorable "grand- kisses" Dakota, Demi, Konner, Levi and Joshua, Jr.

Follow @DrMikeFreeman on all social media networks.